GREAT FISH
COOKBOOK

Consulting Editor:
Valerie Ferguson

HERMES
HOUSE

Contents

Introduction   4

Types of Fish   6

Techniques   8

Soups & Starters   10

Quick & Easy Dishes   18

Midweek Meals   28

Special Occasion Dishes   44

Fish Salads   56

Introduction

Frequently described as the perfect food, fish is packed with protein, has very little carbohydrate and is a good source of vitamins and minerals.

Although healthy eating is a persuasive argument for enjoying fish, it is only one of many reasons. Fish is the ultimate fast food. It is generally sold prepared, needs very little cooking and, because it has less connective tissue than meat, there is very little shrinkage. It is versatile, lending itself to a wide range of cooking methods, such as poaching, steaming, grilling, frying, braising, baking, roasting and even barbecueing. Try it sauced or in salads, with pasta or as the basis for a risotto or pilaff. Stick it on skewers, toss it in a wok with crisp-tender vegetables or try it packaged in paper. Make it into a pie or a pâté, or enjoy it served simply with a squeeze of lemon juice and a few twists of ground black pepper.

We've trawled the world for the finest fish recipes, from Salmon Teriyaki to Halibut in Lemon Sauce, from Roast Sea Bass to Cajun-style Cod. Within these pages you'll find everything from soups to salads, including quickly prepared meals and stunning dishes for special occasions – an irresistible invitation to eat more fish.

Types of Fish

Explore the wonderful variety of fish in our seas and inland waters. The following are just a selection of those available in the shops.

Flat Fish

Dover sole, regarded by many as the most delicious of flat fish, has a delicate flavour and fine, white flesh. It is frequently fried or grilled whole.

Plaice, sold whole or in fillets, has a greyish-brown skin with bright orange spots and is very mild-tasting.

Halibut and turbot grow much larger and both have an excellent flavour. They are often available in steaks.

Skate, related to the shark, is a delicately flavoured fish with a cartilaginous skeleton. Usually fried in butter, it is also delicious grilled or barbecued.

Round Fish

Cod and haddock are probably the best-known round sea fish. Obtainable whole or in fillets or steaks, they have firm, flaky flesh and a good flavour, and are excellent grilled, fried or baked.

Whiting has an especially delicate flavour and texture.

Coley is excellent in soups and other mixed fish dishes.

Dogfish (rock salmon or rock eel) is firm-fleshed and makes good fish stews.

Monkfish has firm, meaty flesh with a taste reminiscent of lobster. It is good for roasting and kebabs as it holds its shape well during cooking.

Above: Fish can be bought as steaks, fillets or whole for cooking.

Red mullet has delicate white flesh and is often grilled or baked whole.

Sea bass is a silvery fish with an excellent flavour and texture. It is usually baked or poached whole.

Swordfish, usually sold in steaks, is ideal for barbecueing, poaching, steaming and baking.

Tuna is a very large, meaty fish. Fresh tuna has a robust flavour. Canned tuna tastes more mellow and is popular for salads and sauces.

Oily round sea fish include anchovies, herring, mackerel and sardines. They are beneficial to health in that the fatty acids they contain help to prevent coronary heart disease.

Salmon is deservedly held in high regard: the firm flesh has a wonderful flavour. It can be cooked by most methods and is truly delectable poached, baked or barbecued whole.

Trout is a freshwater fish that is delicious fried, grilled or baked.

Above: A selection of fish and shellfish available from the fishmonger.

Carp, a red freshwater fish, can taste rather muddy, so it is best incorporated into a mixed fish dish with a well-flavoured sauce.

Pike is a freshwater fish easily recognized by its long, sharp head. The white, flaky flesh is excellent for stuffings and quenelles.

Smoked fish, including salmon, trout, haddock, herring and mackerel, is delicious on its own or combined with other ingredients.

Shellfish

Mussels, available all year round, have a wonderful, sweet flavour and can be eaten steamed, baked with a stuffing or added to sauces and salads.

Prawns are also sweet-fleshed, and very versatile, combining well with many other kinds of fish.

Techniques

Preparing Whole Fish

1 To scale a fish, grasp the tail firmly and scrape off the scales using a fish scaler or a knife. Work from the tail towards the head. Rinse the fish well. Repeat on the other side.

2 Before cooking whole fish, slit along the belly using a sharp knife. Scrape out the entrails and rinse the fish thoroughly under cold running water.

3 For flat fish to be cooked whole, use kitchen scissors to trim off the outer half of the small fin bones.

4 For round fish, cut the flesh on both sides of the anal and dorsal (back) fins and pull them out; the small bones attached will come out too. Trim off the other fins.

5 If the fish is to be cooked whole, leave the fins on, or just trim them, because they help keep the shape of the fish. If the tail is to be left on, cut a neat "V" in the centre with scissors. The fish is now ready for cooking.

Filleting a Round Fish

Cut off the head. With the tip of a knife, cut through the skin all along the length of the backbone. Working from head to tail, use short strokes to cut one fillet off the rib bones in one piece. Cut across the tail to release the fillet. Repeat for the other fillet.

Filleting a Flat Fish

Make an incision in the skin around the head, then cut down the centre of one side of the fish. Working from the head end, and from the centre outwards, scrape the flesh off the bones to ease the first fillet away in one piece. Repeat with the remaining three fillets.

Skinning a Fish Fillet

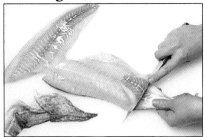

Lay the fillet flat, skin-side down, tail end towards you. Cut across the tail end, through to the skin. Grip the bit of skin and insert the knife blade so it is almost parallel to the skin. Cut the fillet away using a sawing motion.

Skinning a Whole Flat Fish

Lay the fish on a flat surface and cut through the skin just above the tail. Ease enough skin away to get a grip, then pull it off. Repeat on the second side. To get a firm grip, you may find it helpful to salt your fingers.

COOK'S TIPS:
• Different types of fish can be mixed in soups and stews to create sensational flavours. Try a mixture of white fish with smoked fish fillets and prawns.
• When poaching whole fish, start with cold water to preserve the shape of the skin; add fillets or steaks to simmering liquid.
• To calculate how much fish to buy, allow about 150–175 g/5–6 oz fish fillets or 175–200 g/6–7 oz fish steaks per person.

Peeling & Cleaning Prawns

1 Pull off the head, slit or pull the shell apart along the underside between the legs, then use your thumbs to slip it off and release the tail.

2 Straighten the prawn, then carefully pull out the vein from the head end. If it breaks off, use a sharp knife to make a small cut down the back to remove the rest. Rinse and pat dry with kitchen paper.

Cleaning Mussels

1 Discard any mussels with cracked or broken shells, also any shells which are not tightly closed or which do not snap shut when tapped. Scrub the shells and remove the hairy "beard" which sticks out from the shell. Rinse under running water.

2 If you have harvested the mussels yourself, leave them in a large bucket of sea water for several hours, changing the water once or twice so that they expel any sand.

Italian Fish Soup

In this Ligurian dish, the fish are cooked in a broth with vegetables and then puréed. This soup can also be used to dress pasta.

Serves 6

INGREDIENTS

1 kg/2¼ lb mixed fish or fish pieces (such as
    coley, dogfish, whiting, red mullet, cod)
90 ml/6 tbsp olive oil, plus extra to serve
1 medium onion, finely chopped
1 celery stick, chopped
1 carrot, chopped
60 ml/4 tbsp chopped fresh parsley
175 ml/6 fl oz/¾ cup dry white wine
3 medium tomatoes, peeled and chopped
2 garlic cloves, finely chopped
1.5 litres/2½ pints/6¼ cups boiling water
salt and freshly ground black pepper
rounds of French bread, to serve

3 Pour in the wine, raise the heat and cook until it reduces by about half. Stir in the tomatoes and garlic. Cook for 3–4 minutes, stirring occasionally. Pour in the boiling water and bring back to the boil. Cook over moderate heat for 15 minutes.

4 Stir in the fish and simmer for 10–15 minutes or until the fish are tender. Season with salt and pepper.

1 Scale and clean the fish, discarding all innards, but leaving the heads on. Cut into large pieces. Rinse well.

2 Heat the oil in a large saucepan and add the onion. Cook over low to moderate heat until it begins to soften. Stir in the celery and carrot and cook for 5 minutes more. Add the parsley.

5 Remove the fish from the soup with a slotted spoon and discard any bones. Return the fish to the soup and purée in a food processor. Season to taste. Add a little more water if necessary.

6 To serve, heat the soup to simmering. Toast the rounds of bread, and sprinkle with olive oil. Place two or three rounds in each soup plate before pouring over the soup.

VARIATION: To use the soup as a pasta dressing, cook until it reduces to the consistency of a sauce.

Fish Soup with Dumplings

This substantial Czech soup takes little time to make compared with a meat-based one. Use a variety of whatever fish is available.

Serves 4–8

INGREDIENTS
3 rindless bacon rashers, diced
675 g/1½ lb mixed fish (such as perch,
    dogfish, cod, snapper, carp), skinned,
    boned and diced
15 ml/1 tbsp paprika, plus extra
    to garnish
1.5 litres/2½ pints/6¼ cups fish stock
    or water
3 firm tomatoes, peeled and chopped
4 waxy potatoes, peeled and grated
5–10 ml/1–2 tsp chopped
    fresh marjoram
fresh marjoram, to garnish

FOR THE DUMPLINGS
75 g/3 oz/½ cup semolina
    or flour
1 egg, beaten
45 ml/3 tbsp milk or water
generous pinch of salt
15 ml/1 tbsp chopped
    fresh parsley

1 Dry fry the diced bacon in a large pan until pale golden brown, then add the fish. Fry for 1–2 minutes, taking care not to break up the pieces of fish.

2 Sprinkle in the paprika, then pour in the fish stock or water. Bring the mixture to the boil, then reduce the heat and simmer for 10 minutes.

3 Stir the tomatoes, grated potato and marjoram into the pan. Cook for 10 minutes, stirring occasionally.

4 Meanwhile, to make the dumplings, mix all the ingredients together, then leave to stand, covered with clear film, for 5–10 minutes.

5 Drop spoonfuls of the dumpling mixture into the simmering soup and cook for 10 minutes. Serve hot, sprinkled with a few leaves of marjoram and paprika.

Haddock Chowder

A tasty, warming soup for hearty appetites.

Serves 4

INGREDIENTS
4 spring onions, sliced
450 g/1 lb new potatoes, diced
300 ml/½ pint/1¼ cups fish stock or water
300 ml/½ pint/1¼ cups skimmed milk
1 bay leaf
225 g/8 oz/2 cups broccoli florets, sliced
450 g/1 lb smoked haddock fillets, skinned
200 g/7 oz can sweetcorn, drained
freshly ground black pepper
chopped spring onions, to garnish
crusty bread, to serve

1 Place the sliced spring onions with the potatoes in a large saucepan and add the fish stock or water, milk and bay leaf.

2 Bring to the boil, then cover the pan and simmer for 10 minutes. Add the broccoli to the pan. Cut the fish into bite-size chunks and add to the pan with the sweetcorn.

3 Season the soup well with black pepper, then cover the pan and simmer for a further 5 minutes or until the fish is cooked through. Remove the bay leaf and scatter over the chopped spring onions. Serve hot, with crusty bread.

VARIATION: When new potatoes are not available, old ones can be used for this recipe, but choose a waxy variety which will not disintegrate during cooking.

Potted Salmon with Dill

This sophisticated starter would be ideal for a dinner party.

Serves 6

INGREDIENTS
350 g/12 oz cooked salmon, skinned
90 g/3½ oz/6 tbsp butter, softened
rind and juice of 1 large lemon
5 ml/1 tsp chopped fresh dill
75 g/3 oz/¾ cup flaked almonds, roughly
    chopped
salt and freshly ground black pepper
dill sprigs, to garnish
crudités, to serve

1 Flake the salmon into a bowl and then place in a food processor together with the butter, the lemon rind and juice, the dill and seasoning. Process until quite smooth.

2 Mix in the chopped flaked almonds. Check the seasoning and add salt and freshly ground black pepper to taste. Pack the mixture into six small ramekins.

3 Chill the pâté before serving, garnished with sprigs of dill. Serve with a selection of crudités.

Marinated Anchovies

Fresh anchovies are tiny, so be prepared to spend time filleting them – the results will be worth the effort.

Serves 4

INGREDIENTS
225 g/8 oz fresh anchovies
juice of 3 lemons
30 ml/2 tbsp extra-virgin olive oil
2 garlic cloves, finely chopped
15 ml/1 tbsp chopped fresh parsley
flaked sea salt

1 Cut off the heads and tails from the anchovies, then split them open down one side. Open each fish out flat and carefully lift out the bone. Arrange the anchovies skin-side down in a single layer on a plate. Pour over two-thirds of the lemon juice and sprinkle with salt.

2 Cover and leave for at least 1 or up to 24 hours, basting occasionally with the juices, until the flesh is white and no longer translucent.

3 Transfer the fish to a serving plate and drizzle over the olive oil and the remaining lemon juice. Scatter over the garlic and parsley, cover and chill until ready to serve.

COOK'S TIP: The lemon juice used for the marinade tenderizes and cooks the fish in this Spanish tapas recipe.

Dover Sole Goujons

This sweet-fleshed fish is ideal for making into goujons. Serve them with a quickly prepared tartare sauce.

Serves 4

INGREDIENTS
675 g/1½ lb Dover sole fillets
175 g/6 oz/3 cups
  white breadcrumbs
15 ml/1 tbsp chopped
  fresh tarragon
2 eggs, lightly beaten
lemon wedges, to serve

FOR THE SAUCE
15 ml/1 tbsp capers, drained
15 ml/1 tbsp gherkins, drained
150 ml/¼ pint/⅔ cup mayonnaise
salt and freshly ground
  black pepper

1 Preheat the oven to 220°C/ 425°F/Gas 7. Cut the fish fillets into thin strips. In a bowl, stir the breadcrumbs and tarragon together until thoroughly mixed.

2 Dip the fish strips into the egg and then into the breadcrumb mixture, ensuring that they are well coated. Place on a greased baking sheet and cook in the oven for 10 minutes.

3 To make the sauce, roughly chop the capers and gherkins and stir into the mayonnaise. Season to taste and serve with the crispy goujons and the lemon wedges.

Salmon Teriyaki

Marinating the salmon makes it so wonderfully tender that it just melts in the mouth, and the crunchy condiment provides an excellent foil.

Serves 4

INGREDIENTS
675 g/1½ lb salmon fillet
30 ml/2 tbsp sunflower oil
watercress, to garnish

FOR THE TERIYAKI SAUCE
5 ml/1 tsp caster sugar
5 ml/1 tsp dry white wine
5 ml/1 tsp rice wine or dry sherry
30 ml/2 tbsp dark soy sauce

FOR THE CONDIMENT
5 cm/2 in piece fresh root ginger,
    peeled and grated
few drops of pink food colouring
50 g/2 oz mooli, grated

2 Skin the salmon, cut it into strips, then place it in a non-metallic dish. Pour over the teriyaki sauce and leave to marinate for 10–15 minutes.

3 To make the condiment, place the ginger in a bowl, mix in the food colouring, then stir in the mooli.

4 Lift the salmon carefully from the teriyaki sauce and drain in a sieve placed over a bowl.

1 To make the teriyaki sauce, place all the ingredients in a bowl and stir until the sugar dissolves.

VARIATION: If you are short of time, you can use a good, bottled teriyaki sauce.

5 Heat a wok, then add the oil. When the oil is hot, add the salmon and stir-fry in batches for 3–4 minutes until it is cooked through. Garnish with watercress and serve with the mooli and ginger condiment.

Grilled Red Mullet

This recipe is very simple – the taste of grilled red mullet is so good in itself that it needs very little to bring out the flavour.

Serves 4

INGREDIENTS

4 red mullet (about 275 g/10 oz each), cleaned
4 garlic cloves, cut lengthways into thin slivers
75 ml/5 tbsp olive oil
30 ml/2 tbsp balsamic vinegar
10 ml/2 tsp very finely chopped fresh
   rosemary or 5 ml/1 tsp dried rosemary
coarse sea salt and freshly ground
   black pepper
fresh rosemary sprigs and lemon wedges,
   to garnish

1 Cut three diagonal slits in both sides of each fish. Push the garlic slivers into the slits. Place the fish in a single layer in a shallow dish.

2 In a bowl, whisk together the oil, vinegar and rosemary, with ground black pepper to taste. Pour the mixture over the fish, cover with clear film and leave to marinate in a cool place for about 1 hour.

3 Place the fish on the rack of a grill pan and grill for 5–6 minutes on each side, turning once and brushing with the marinade. Serve hot, sprinkled with coarse sea salt and garnished with fresh rosemary sprigs and lemon wedges.

VARIATION: Red mullet, marinated this way, are extra-delicious cooked on a barbecue.

Fish Parcels

A method of cooking fish in hot embers traditionally used by fishermen, the parcels seal in all the wonderful flavour and aroma.

Serves 4

INGREDIENTS
4 small trout (about 400 g/14 oz each)
juice of 1 lemon
50 g/2 oz/4 tbsp butter, melted
½ fennel bulb, cut into strips
few sprigs of fresh parsley or dill
salt and freshly ground black pepper or
   cayenne pepper
cornbread, and tomato and cucumber salad,
   to serve

1 Preheat the oven to 180°C/350°F/ Gas 4 or light the barbecue. Remove the heads, tails, fins and scales from the fish. Rinse and pat dry. Season well and sprinkle with lemon juice.

2 Cut out four double sheets of greaseproof or baking paper, large enough to enclose each fish. Brush each fish with the melted butter and place in the centre. Sprinkle with the fennel and half of the herbs.

3 Wrap up the fish loosely to make four neat parcels. Press down the edges securely. Bake in the oven for about 15–20 minutes, depending on the thickness of the fish, or for 20–30 minutes, if cooking on a barbecue.

4 Transfer the fish to serving plates and peel back the paper. Garnish with the remaining herbs and serve with cornbread and salad.

Seafood Pilaff

A one-pot main course suitable for any day of the week.

Serves 4

INGREDIENTS
10 ml/2 tsp olive oil
250 g/9 oz/1¼ cups long grain rice
5 ml/1 tsp ground turmeric
1 red pepper, seeded and diced
1 small onion, finely chopped
2 medium courgettes, sliced
150 g/5 oz/2 cups button mushrooms, halved
350 ml/12 fl oz/1½ cups fish or
    chicken stock
150 ml/¼ pint/⅔ cup orange juice
350 g/12 oz white fish fillets, cut into
    large pieces
12 fresh mussels in the shell, cleaned
salt and freshly ground black pepper
grated rind of 1 orange, to garnish

1 Heat the oil in a large, non-stick pan and fry the rice and turmeric over a low heat for about 1 minute.

2 Add the red pepper, onion, courgettes and mushrooms. Stir in the fish or chicken stock and orange juice. Bring to the boil.

3 Reduce the heat and add the fish. Cover and simmer gently for about 15 minutes until the rice is tender and the liquid absorbed. Stir in the mussels and cook until they open; discard any that remain closed. Season to taste, sprinkle with orange rind and serve.

Salmon Pasta

The delicious sauce for this dish is prepared in seconds.

Serves 4

INGREDIENTS
450 g/1 lb salmon fillet, skinned
225 g/8 oz/3 cups pasta, such as penne
    or twists
175 g/6 oz cherry tomatoes, halved
150 ml/¼ pint/⅔ cup
    crème fraîche
45 ml/3 tbsp finely
    chopped parsley
finely grated rind of ½ orange
salt and freshly ground
    black pepper

1 Cut the salmon into bite-size pieces, arrange on a heatproof plate and cover with foil.

2 Bring a large pan of salted water to the boil, add the pasta and return to the boil. Place the plate of salmon on top and simmer for 10–12 minutes, until the pasta and salmon are cooked.

3 Drain the pasta and toss with the tomatoes and salmon in a large bowl. In a small bowl, mix together the crème fraîche, parsley, orange rind and pepper to taste, then toss into the pasta. Serve hot or cold.

*Right: Seafood Pilaff (top);
Salmon Pasta*

Cod Fillet with a Herb Crust

Mixed fresh herbs make a delicious topping for baked fish.

Serves 4

INGREDIENTS

15 ml/1 tbsp fresh chervil
15 ml/1 tbsp fresh parsley
15 ml/1 tbsp fresh chives
25 g/1 oz/2 tbsp butter
175 g/6 oz/3 cups wholemeal breadcrumbs
4 x 225 g/8 oz thickly cut cod
  fillets, skinned
15 ml/1 tbsp olive oil
salt and freshly ground black pepper
fresh herbs, to garnish

1 Preheat the oven to 200°C/400°F/ Gas 6. Finely chop the herbs. Melt the butter and mix with the breadcrumbs. Stir in the herbs and seasoning.

2 Lay the cod fillets on a baking sheet and press a quarter of the herb mixture on top of each one. Drizzle over the olive oil.

3 Bake in the oven for 15 minutes until the fish flesh is firm and the top turns golden. Serve garnished with fresh herbs.

Whiting Fillets in a Polenta Coating

Give fried fish a wonderful crunchy texture with this unusual coating.

Serves 4

INGREDIENTS
8 small whiting fillets
finely grated rind of 1 lemon
225 g/8 oz/2 cups polenta
30 ml/2 tbsp olive oil
15 ml/1 tbsp butter
30 ml/2 tbsp chopped mixed fresh herbs such
    as parsley, chervil and chives
salt and freshly ground black pepper
steamed spinach topped with red onion slices
    and toasted pine nuts, to serve

1 Make four small cuts in the skin of each fillet. Sprinkle with the seasoning and lemon rind. Press the polenta on to the fish. Chill for 15 minutes.

2 Heat the oil and butter in a large frying pan and gently fry the fillets on each side for 3–4 minutes until just cooked through.

3 Sprinkle the fish with chopped herbs and serve immediately with steamed spinach topped with red onion slices and toasted pine nuts.

Trout with Almonds

Cook the trout in two frying pans or in batches, if preferred.

Serves 2

INGREDIENTS
2 trout (about 350 g/12 oz each), cleaned
40 g/1½ oz/⅓ cup plain flour
50 g/2 oz/4 tbsp butter
25 g/1 oz/¼ cup flaked almonds
30 ml/2 tbsp dry white wine
salt and freshly ground black pepper

1 Rinse the trout and pat dry. Put the flour in a large polythene bag and season with salt and pepper. Place the trout, one at a time, in the bag and shake to coat with flour.

2 Melt half the butter in a large frying pan over medium heat. When it is foamy, add the trout and cook for 6–7 minutes on each side until golden brown and the flesh next to the bone is opaque. Transfer the fish to warmed plates and cover to keep warm.

3 Add the remaining butter to the pan and cook the almonds until just lightly browned. Add the wine to the pan and boil for 1 minute, stirring constantly, until slightly syrupy. Pour or spoon over the fish and serve.

*Right: Trout with Almonds (top);
Tuna with Tomatoes*

Tuna with Tomatoes

The tomato and garlic sauce complements the rich fish perfectly.

Serves 4

INGREDIENTS
4 tuna steaks, about 2.5 cm/1 in thick
    (175–200 g/6–7 oz each)
30–45 ml/2–3 tbsp olive oil
3 or 4 garlic cloves, finely chopped
60 ml/4 tbsp dry white wine
3 plum tomatoes, peeled, seeded and chopped
5 ml/1 tsp dried herbes de Provence
salt and freshly ground black pepper
fresh basil leaves, to garnish
scalloped potatoes, to serve

1 Season the tuna steaks with salt and pepper. Set a heavy frying pan over high heat until very hot, add the oil and swirl to coat. Add the tuna steaks and press down gently, then reduce the heat to medium and cook for 6–8 minutes, turning once, until just slightly pink in the centre.

2 Transfer the fish to a serving plate and cover to keep warm. Add the garlic to the pan and fry for 15-20 seconds, stirring, then pour in the wine and boil until it is reduced by half.

3 Add the tomatoes and herbs and cook for 2–3 minutes. Season and pour over the fish steaks. Garnish with basil and serve with scalloped potatoes.

Cajun-style Cod

This recipe works equally well with any firm-fleshed fish such as swordfish, shark, tuna or halibut.

Serves 4

INGREDIENTS
4 cod steaks (about 175 g/6 oz each)
30 ml/2 tbsp plain yogurt
15 ml/1 tbsp lime or
    lemon juice
1 garlic clove, crushed
5 ml/1 tsp ground cumin
5 ml/1 tsp paprika
5 ml/1 tsp mustard powder
2.5 ml/½ tsp cayenne pepper
2.5 ml/½ tsp dried thyme
2.5 ml/½ tsp dried oregano
vegetable oil, for cooking
lemon slices, to garnish
new potatoes and mixed salad leaves,
    to serve

2 Mix together the garlic, spices and herbs. Coat both sides of the fish with the seasoning mix, rubbing in well.

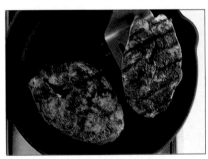

3 Lightly oil a ridged grill pan or heavy-based frying pan and heat until very hot. Add the fish and cook over a high heat for 4 minutes or until the underside is well browned.

1 Pat the fish dry on absorbent kitchen paper. Mix together the yogurt and lime or lemon juice, and brush lightly over both sides of the fish.

VARIATION: If you don't have a ridged grill pan you can give the fish a ridged appearance. Heat several metal skewers under a grill until red hot, hold the ends with a cloth and press on to the fish before cooking.

4 Turn over and cook for a further 4 minutes or until the steaks have cooked through. Serve immediately, garnished with lemon slices and accompanied by new potatoes and mixed salad leaves.

Halibut in Lemon Sauce

The delicately flavoured sauce is made using the stock in which the fish is poached and is well worth the small effort required.

Serves 4

INGREDIENTS
1 small onion
1 large carrot
300 ml/½ pint/1¼ cups water
2.5 ml/½ tsp sugar
4 halibut steaks
    (about 175 g/6 oz each)
2 lemons
3 egg yolks
salt and freshly ground
    black pepper
asparagus and new potatoes,
    to serve

1 Slice the onion and carrot and bring to the boil with the water in a wide pan. Season with sugar, salt and black pepper and simmer for 15 minutes. Remove the vegetable pieces with a slotted spoon and put aside. Lower the halibut steaks into the cooking liquid and cook over low heat for about 8 minutes.

COOK'S TIPS: When buying halibut steaks avoid those from the tail end as they can be dry.
    Lightly poaching halibut, as in this recipe, is an ideal way to preserve its flavour and texture.

2 Insert a knife near the bone of the halibut steaks: if the fish looks opaque, it is cooked. Lift the steaks out and arrange them on a shallow dish. Cover with foil if you want to serve them hot. Bring the cooking liquid to the boil again and reduce it over a high heat for a few minutes.

3 To make the lemon sauce cut a few slices from each lemon and set them aside for garnishing, if you wish. Squeeze the juice from the remaining pieces of lemon, whisk the egg yolks in a bowl and stir in the lemon juice.

4 Strain the reduced cooking liquid on to the egg and lemon mixture and return to the pan. Stir over a very low heat without boiling until thickened.

5 Pour it over the fish and serve hot or cold, garnished with lemon slices, if using, accompanied by asparagus and new potatoes.

31

Poached Skate & Black Butter

This classic dish can be prepared with or without the capers.

Serves 4

INGREDIENTS
1 litre/1¾ pints/4 cups water
1 carrot, sliced
1 small onion, sliced
1 bouquet garni
6 peppercorns
120 ml/4 fl oz/½ cup white
  wine vinegar
5 ml/1 tsp salt
8 skate wings
freshly ground black pepper
fresh herbs, to garnish

FOR THE BLACK BUTTER
115 g/4 oz/½ cup butter
30 ml/2 tbsp drained capers

1 Place the water, carrot, onion, bouquet garni, peppercorns, 75 ml/3 fl oz/⅓ cup of the vinegar and the salt into a large, heavy-based saucepan. Bring to the boil and simmer, uncovered, for 20 minutes.

2 Lower the skate wings into the liquid and poach for about 10 minutes until cooked through. Carefully lift the fish from the pan, drain and keep warm.

3 Meanwhile, to make the black butter, heat the butter in a pan until it turns brown. Remove from the heat and stir in the capers. Pour the butter over the skate and season with pepper. Deglaze the pan with the remaining vinegar and pour on top. Serve immediately garnished with herbs.

Coconut Salmon

The fish is marinated with spices and gently poached in coconut milk.

Serves 4

INGREDIENTS
10 ml/2 tsp ground cumin
10 ml/2 tsp chilli powder
2.5 ml/½ tsp ground turmeric
30 ml/2 tbsp white wine vinegar
1.5 ml/¼ tsp salt
4 salmon steaks (about 175 g/6 oz each)
45 ml/3 tbsp oil
1 onion, chopped
2 green chillies, seeded and chopped
2 garlic cloves, crushed
2.5 cm/1 in piece fresh root ginger, peeled and grated
5 ml/1 tsp ground coriander
175 ml/6 fl oz/¾ cup coconut milk
fresh coriander sprigs, to garnish
spring onion rice, to serve

1 Mix 5 ml/1 tsp of the ground cumin together with the chilli powder, turmeric, vinegar and salt. Rub the paste over the salmon steaks and leave to marinate for about 15 minutes.

2 Heat the oil in a frying pan and fry the onion, chillies, garlic and ginger for 5–6 minutes. Transfer to a food processor and process to a paste.

3 Return the paste to the pan. Add the remaining cumin, the ground coriander and coconut milk. Bring to the boil and simmer for 5 minutes. Add the salmon steaks. Cover and cook for 15 minutes until the fish is tender. Serve with spring onion rice and garnish with fresh coriander.

Mediterranean Baked Fish

This informal fish bake is said to have originated with the fishermen on the Côte d'Azur who would cook the remains of their catch for lunch in the still-warm baker's oven.

Serves 4

INGREDIENTS
3 medium potatoes
2 onions, halved and sliced
30 ml/2 tbsp olive oil, plus extra
    for drizzling
2 garlic cloves, very finely chopped
675 g/1½ lb thick skinless fish fillets,
    such as turbot or sea bass
1 bay leaf
1 fresh thyme sprig
3 tomatoes, peeled and
    thinly sliced
30 ml/2 tbsp orange juice
60 ml/4 tbsp dry white wine
2.5 ml/½ tsp saffron threads,
    soaked in 60 ml/4 tbsp boiling water
salt and freshly ground
    black pepper

1 Cook the potatoes in boiling salted water for 15 minutes, then drain. When the potatoes are cool enough to handle, peel them and slice thinly.

2 Meanwhile, in a heavy-based frying pan, fry the onions in the oil over medium-low heat for about 10 minutes, stirring frequently. Add the garlic and continue cooking for a few minutes until the onions are soft and golden.

3 Preheat the oven to 190°C/375°F/ Gas 5. Layer half the potato slices in a 2 litres/3½ pints/8¾ cups baking dish. Cover with half the onions. Season with salt and pepper.

4 Place the fish fillets on top of the vegetables and tuck the herbs in between them. Top with the tomato slices and then the remaining onions and potatoes.

5 Pour over the orange juice, wine and saffron liquid, season with salt and pepper and drizzle a little olive oil on top. Bake, uncovered, for about 25-30 minutes until the potatoes are tender and the fish is cooked. Serve hot.

Fried Fish

A traditional Jewish dish, nearly always served cold. If you have never tried it, you are missing a real speciality. A tray of different fish is usual, but you can use one variety if you prefer.

Serves 8

INGREDIENTS
2 Dover sole (about 225 g/8 oz each)
2 large plaice (about 450 g/1 lb each)
1 thick cod fillet
   (about 450 g/1 lb), skinned
1.5 litres/2½ pints/6¼ cups oil,
   for frying
45 ml/3 tbsp flour
40–50 g/1½–2 oz/8–10 tbsp
   medium-ground matzo meal
4 eggs
salt and freshly ground
   black pepper
lemon slices, to garnish
potato salad and pickled cucumbers,
   to serve

1 Wash the fish and dry thoroughly. Leave the Dover sole whole, but cut the plaice across the main bone in the centre into three sections. Cut the cod fillet into two or three pieces.

2 Start heating the oil in a large, deep pan. It will take 4–6 minutes for 2.5 cm/1 in of oil to reach a hot enough temperature (190°C/375°F). If you do not have a thermometer, drop a cube of bread into the oil and it should brown in 30 seconds.

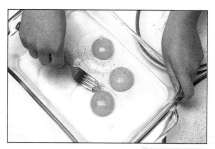

3 Put the flour and matzo meal on separate plates and the eggs in a glass dish. Season the matzo meal and the eggs. Beat the eggs.

4 Dip each piece of fish first into the flour and then into the beaten egg. Lift it out immediately and dip it into the matzo meal.

5 Lower the fish into the hot oil. Don't put in too many pieces together as this reduces the temperature of the oil. Fry for about 6 minutes. Turn the fish over and, when it is crisp and brown, lift it out with a slotted spoon.

6 Drain the fish over the oil and leave to cool on kitchen paper. Serve, garnished with lemon slices with potato salad and pickled cucumbers.

COOK'S TIPS: Use corn or sunflower oil for frying fish. A wok is useful for deep frying.

Green Fish Curry

All the flavours of the East are captured in this spicy dish, which can be made with cod, as here, or any firm, white fish.

Serves 4

INGREDIENTS
1.5 ml/¼ tsp ground turmeric
30 ml/2 tbsp lime juice
4 cod fillets, skinned and cut into
    5 cm/2 in chunks
1 onion, chopped
1 green chilli, roughly chopped
1 garlic clove, crushed
25 g/1 oz/¼ cup cashew nuts
2.5 ml/½ tsp fennel seeds
30 ml/2 tbsp desiccated coconut
30 ml/2 tbsp oil
1.5 ml/¼ tsp cumin seeds
1.5 ml/¼ tsp ground coriander
1.5 ml/¼ tsp ground cumin
150 ml/¼ pint/⅔ cup water
175 ml/6 fl oz/¾ cup single cream
45 ml/3 tbsp finely chopped
    fresh coriander
salt
rice with peas, to serve
fresh coriander sprig, to garnish

1 Mix together the turmeric, lime juice and a pinch of salt and rub over the fish. Cover and leave to marinate for 15 minutes.

COOK'S TIP: For the rice, add peas, sweetcorn and chopped red peppers to boiled rice towards the end of the cooking time.

2 Meanwhile put the onion, chilli, garlic, cashew nuts, fennel seeds and coconut in a food processor or blender and process to a paste. Spoon the paste into a bowl and set aside.

3 Heat the oil in a large frying pan and fry the cumin seeds for 2 minutes until they begin to splutter. Add the paste and fry for 5 minutes, then stir in the ground coriander, cumin, 1.5 ml/ ¼ tsp salt and the water and cook for about 2–3 minutes.

4 Add the cream and the fresh coriander. Simmer for 5 minutes. Add the fish and gently stir in. Cover and cook gently for 10 minutes until the fish is tender. Serve accompanied by rice with peas, garnished with a coriander sprig.

Fish Goulash

This wholesome dish is a cross between a stew and a soup.

Serves 6

INGREDIENTS
2 kg/4½ lb mixed fish
4 large onions, sliced
2 garlic cloves, crushed
½ small celeriac, diced
handful of parsley stalks or cleaned roots
30 ml/2 tbsp paprika
1 green pepper, seeded and sliced
5–10 ml/1–2 tsp tomato purée
salt
90 ml/6 tbsp soured cream, fennel seeds and
  3 cherry peppers, to serve

1 Skin and fillet the fish and cut the flesh into chunks. Put all the fish heads, skin and bones into a large pan, together with the onions, garlic, celeriac, parsley, paprika and salt. Cover with water and bring to the boil. Reduce the heat and simmer for 1¼–1½ hours. Strain the stock.

2 Place the fish and green pepper in a large frying pan and pour over the stock. Blend the tomato purée with a little stock and add it to the pan. Heat gently but do not stir. Cook for 10–12 minutes without boiling. Season to taste. Ladle into bowls and top with soured cream, some fennel seeds and half a cherry pepper.

Right: Fish Goulash (top); Fish Sausages

Fish Sausages

A Hungarian recipe which dates back to the 17th century.

Serves 3–4

INGREDIENTS
375 g/13 oz fish fillets, such as perch, pike,
  carp or cod, skinned
1 white bread roll
75 ml/5 tbsp milk
25 ml/1½ tbsp chopped fresh flat leaf parsley
2 eggs, well beaten
50 g/2 oz/½ cup plain flour
50 g/2 oz/1 cup fine fresh white breadcrumbs
oil, for shallow frying
salt and freshly ground black pepper
deep fried sprigs of parsley and lemon
  wedges sprinkled with paprika, to serve

1 Mince or process the fish coarsely in a mincer or food processor. Soak the roll in the milk for about 10 minutes, then squeeze it out. Mix the fish and bread together, then add the parsley, half the beaten egg and seasoning.

2 Using your fingers, shape the mixture into 10 cm/4 in long sausages, about 2.5 cm/1 in thick. Carefully roll the fish "sausages" in the flour, then in the remaining beaten egg and lastly in the breadcrumbs.

3 Heat the oil in a pan and slowly cook the "sausages" until golden brown all over. Drain on kitchen paper. Serve garnished with parsley sprigs and lemon wedges.

Swordfish Kebabs

The firm, meaty flesh of swordfish is ideal for these delicious kebabs, which may be grilled or barbecued.

Serves 4

INGREDIENTS
900 g/2 lb swordfish, skinned
5 ml/1 tsp paprika, plus extra to garnish
60 ml/4 tbsp lemon juice
45 ml/3 tbsp olive oil
6 fresh bay leaves, plus extra to garnish
4 small tomatoes
2 green peppers, seeded and cut into
    5 cm/2 in pieces
2 onions, cut into 4 wedges each
salt and freshly ground white pepper
lettuce leaves, soured cream, cucumber salad
    and lime or lemon wedges, to serve

FOR THE SAUCE
120 ml/4 fl oz/½ cup extra virgin olive oil
juice of 1 lemon
60 ml/4 tbsp finely chopped fresh parsley
salt and freshly ground black pepper

1 Cut the swordfish into 5 cm/2 in cubes and place in a shallow dish. In a small bowl, mix together the paprika, lemon juice, olive oil and seasoning.

2 Pour the mixture over the fish. Crush two bay leaves and sprinkle over the top. Cover and chill for at least 2 hours, carefully turning the fish cubes in the marinade once or twice.

3 Thread the fish and vegetables on four large skewers, finishing each with a bay leaf. Cook under a preheated grill or over a barbecue, basting with any remaining marinade from time to time. Turn the kebabs once during cooking.

4 Meanwhile, to make the sauce, whisk the oil, lemon juice, parsley and seasoning together in a bowl until emulsified. Pour into a jug.

5 Arrange the kebabs on lettuce leaves and serve with the sauce, soured cream sprinkled with paprika, a cucumber salad and lime or lemon wedges. Garnish with extra bay leaves, if liked.

COOK'S TIP: Keep the root end intact when preparing the onion, so that the wedges will hold together during cooking.

43

Monkfish with Asparagus & Pears

A superb, firm-fleshed fish, monkfish has a flavour that is often likened to that of lobster.

Serves 4

INGREDIENTS
15 ml/1 tbsp sunflower oil
knob of butter, for flavouring (optional)
1 medium onion, sliced
1 garlic clove, crushed
2 courgettes, diagonally sliced
2 firm dessert pears, cored
    and sliced
675 g/1½ lb monkfish tail, skinned, boned
    and cut into chunks
175 ml/6 fl oz/¾ cup medium-dry
    white wine or cider
175 ml/6 fl oz/¾ cup fish stock
225 g/8 oz asparagus
    spears, trimmed
strip of pared lemon rind
few fresh dill sprigs
45 ml/3 tbsp soured cream or
    crème fraîche
10 ml/2 tsp cornflour
salt and freshly ground
    black pepper

1 Heat the oil and the butter, if using, in a large frying pan. Cook the onion, garlic, courgettes and pears over a gentle heat for about 5 minutes until the onion is just beginning to brown. Using a slotted spoon, transfer the mixture to a plate.

2 Add the monkfish chunks to the fat remaining in the pan and cook for 2–3 minutes, turning frequently, until lightly browned on both sides.

3 Pour in the wine or cider and fish stock and return the vegetables and fruit to the pan.

4 Add the asparagus spears and lemon rind. Season with salt and pepper. Bring to the boil, then lower the heat, cover the pan and simmer gently for about 8 minutes.

5 Reserve a little of the dill for the garnish and add the rest to the pan. Cover and simmer for 4–7 minutes more, until both fish and asparagus are tender. Discard the dill and, using a slotted spoon, remove the fish, fruit and vegetables to a warmed serving dish and keep hot.

6 Mix the soured cream or crème fraîche with the cornflour in a small bowl, then stir into the juices remaining in the pan. Cook over a gentle heat, stirring constantly, until thickened. Pour the sauce over the fish, garnish with the reserved dill and serve immediately.

Seafood Pie

There are as many variations of this dish as there are fish in the sea. You can use whichever fish and shellfish are available, for this recipe.

Serves 4

INGREDIENTS
450 g/1 lb fish bones, cleaned
6 peppercorns
1 small onion, sliced
1 bay leaf
900 g/2 lb smoked haddock
225 g/8 oz cooked peeled prawns
450 g/1 lb mussels, cleaned
675 g/1½ lb potatoes
65 g/2½ oz/5 tbsp butter
25 g/1 oz/¼ cup plain flour
350 g/12 oz leeks, sliced
115 g/4 oz/1½ cups small button mushrooms, sliced
15 ml/1 tbsp chopped fresh tarragon
15 ml/1 tbsp chopped fresh parsley
salt and freshly ground black pepper
fresh tarragon, to garnish

1 Put the fish bones, peppercorns, onion and bay leaf into a saucepan with 750 ml/1¼ pints/3 cups cold water. Bring to the boil, reduce the heat and simmer for 20 minutes. Remove from the heat and set aside.

2 Meanwhile, put the haddock into a pan with just enough water to cover it. Cover with a piece of buttered paper and simmer for 15 minutes. Drain and cool, then remove the bones and skin and put the flaked fish into a bowl. Add the prawns.

3 Place the mussels in a saucepan with 30 ml/2 tbsp water. Cover and cook over high heat for 5–6 minutes until the mussels have opened. Discard any that have not. Refresh under cold water and remove the shells. Put the cooked mussels into the bowl with the fish and prawns.

4 Boil the potatoes for 20 minutes. Drain and dry over high heat for 1 minute until all traces of moisture have evaporated. Mash with 25 g/1 oz/2 tbsp of the butter.

5 Meanwhile, melt 25 g/1 oz/2 tbsp of the butter in a saucepan. Stir in the flour and cook for 1 minute. Strain the fish stock and measure 600 ml/1 pint/2½ cups. Whisk a little at a time into the roux until smooth. Cook over a gentle heat for 10 minutes. Preheat the oven to 180°C/350°F/Gas 4.

6 Melt the remaining butter in another saucepan, add the leeks and mushrooms and cook for 4–5 minutes without browning. Add to the fish. Stir in the chopped herbs.

7 Fold in the sauce, then transfer to a pie dish. Spoon over the mashed potatoes and cook in the oven for 30 minutes. Garnish with tarragon before serving.

Turbot in Parchment

Serve this dish plain or with a little hollandaise sauce and let each person open their own parcel to savour the aroma.

Serves 4

INGREDIENTS
2 carrots, cut into thin julienne strips
2 courgettes, cut into thin julienne strips
2 leeks, cut into thin julienne strips
1 fennel bulb, cut into thin julienne strips
2 tomatoes, peeled, seeded and diced
30 ml/2 tbsp chopped fresh dill, tarragon or chervil
4 turbot fillets (about 200 g/7 oz each), cut in half
20 ml/4 tsp olive oil
60 ml/4 tbsp white wine or fish stock
salt and freshly ground black pepper

1 Preheat the oven to 190°C/375°F/ Gas 5. Cut four pieces of non-stick baking paper, about 45 cm/18 in long. Fold each piece in half and cut into a heart shape.

COOK'S TIP: The parcels may be assembled up to 4 hours in advance and chilled.

2 Open the paper hearts. Arrange one quarter of each of the vegetables next to the fold of each heart. Sprinkle with salt and pepper and half of the chopped herbs.

3 Arrange two pieces of turbot fillet over each bed of vegetables, overlapping the thin end of one piece with the thicker end of the other. Sprinkle the remaining herbs, the olive oil and wine or stock evenly over the fish.

4 Fold the top half of one of the paper hearts over the fish and vegetables and, beginning at the rounded end, fold the edges of the paper over, twisting and folding to form an airtight packet. Repeat with the remaining three.

5 Slide the parcels on to one or two baking sheets and bake for about 10 minutes, or until the paper is lightly browned and well puffed. Slide each parcel on to a warmed plate and serve.

Bouillabaisse

This dish is delicious served with a rich garlic mayonnaise and plenty of crusty bread to mop up the juices. Use as many varieties of fish and shellfish as you can find.

Serves 4

INGREDIENTS
450 g/1 lb mixed fish fillets, such as red mullet, monkfish, sea bass, mackerel
450 g/1 lb mixed uncooked shellfish, such as mussels and prawns
pinch of saffron strands
60 ml/4 tbsp olive oil
350 g/12 oz onions, roughly chopped
350 g/12 oz fennel, halved and thinly sliced (about 1 small bulb)
10 ml/2 tsp plain flour
400 g/14 oz can chopped tomatoes, strained
3 garlic cloves, crushed
2 bay leaves
30 ml/2 tbsp chopped fresh thyme
pared rind of 1 orange
salt and cayenne pepper
garlic mayonnaise and crusty bread, to serve

1 Wash and skin the fish, if necessary, and cut into large chunks. Clean the shellfish and remove the heads from the prawns.

2 Place the saffron strands in a bowl and pour over 150 ml/¼ pint/⅔ cup boiling water. Leave the saffron to soak for about 20 minutes. Strain.

3 Heat the oil in a large saucepan and add the onions and fennel. Fry gently for 5 minutes or until beginning to soften, stirring occasionally.

4 Stir in the flour. Gradually blend in 750 ml/1¼ pints/3 cups water, the tomatoes, garlic, bay leaves, thyme, orange rind, saffron liquid and seasoning to taste. Bring to the boil.

5 Reduce the heat and add the fish (not the shellfish) and simmer very gently, uncovered, for about 2 minutes.

COOK'S TIP: To make the garlic mayonnaise, add two crushed garlic cloves to 150 ml/¼ pint/⅔ cup mayonnaise and mix.

6 Add the shellfish and cook for a further 2–3 minutes or until all the fish is cooked but still holding its shape. Discard any mussels that have not opened. Adjust the seasoning. Serve in warmed bowls, with a generous spoonful of garlic mayonnaise and plenty of crusty bread.

Roast Sea Bass

Sea bass has meaty flesh. It is an expensive fish, best cooked as simply as possible. Avoid elaborate sauces, which would mask its delicate flavour.

Serves 4

INGREDIENTS
1 fennel bulb with fronds
    (about 275 g/10 oz)
2 lemons
120 ml/4 fl oz/½ cup olive oil
1 small red onion, diced
2 sea bass (about 500 g/1¼ lb each),
    cleaned, with heads left on
120 ml/4 fl oz/½ cup dry
    white wine
salt and freshly ground
    black pepper
lemon slices, to garnish

2 Heat 30 ml/2 tbsp of the oil in a frying pan, add the diced fennel and onion and cook gently, stirring frequently, for about 5 minutes until softened. Remove from the heat.

1 Preheat the oven to 190°C/375°F/ Gas 5. Cut the fronds off the top of the fennel and reserve for the garnish. Cut the fennel bulb lengthways into thin wedges, then into dice. Cut one half lemon into four slices. Squeeze the juice from the remaining lemon half and the other lemon.

3 Make three diagonal slashes on both sides of each sea bass with a sharp knife. Brush a roasting tin generously with oil, add the fish and tuck two lemon slices in each cavity. Scatter the fennel and onion over the fish.

COOK'S TIP: Do not overcook the sea bass as this will dry out the flesh.

4 Whisk together the remaining oil, the lemon juice, and salt and pepper to taste and pour over the fish. Cover with foil and roast for 30 minutes or until the flesh flakes, removing the foil for the last 10 minutes. Discard the lemon slices, transfer the fish to a heated serving platter and keep hot.

5 Put the roasting tin on top of the stove. Add the wine and stir over a medium heat to incorporate all the pan juices. Bring to the boil, stirring continuously, then spoon the juices over the fish. Garnish with the reserved fennel fronds and lemon slices and serve at once.

Salmon Kulebyaka

A Russian festive dish in which a layer of moist salmon and eggs sits on a bed of buttery, dill-flavoured rice, all encased in crisp puff pastry.

Serves 4

INGREDIENTS
50 g/2 oz/4 tbsp butter
1 small onion, finely chopped
175 g/6 oz/1 cup cooked long grain rice
15 ml/1 tbsp chopped fresh dill
15 ml/1 tbsp lemon juice
450 g/1 lb puff pastry, thawed if frozen
450 g/1 lb salmon fillet, skinned and cut into
    5 cm/2 in pieces
3 eggs, hard-boiled and chopped
beaten egg, for sealing and glazing
salt and freshly ground black pepper
watercress, to garnish

1 Preheat the oven to 200°C/400°F/ Gas 6. Melt the butter in a pan, add the onion and cook gently for 10 minutes or until soft. Stir in the cooked rice, dill, lemon juice, salt and pepper.

2 On a lightly floured surface, roll out the pastry to a 30 cm/12 in square. Spoon the rice mixture over half the pastry, leaving a 2.5 cm/1 in border.

3 Arrange the salmon on top of the rice mixture, then scatter the hard-boiled eggs in between. Brush the edges of the pastry with beaten egg and fold it over the filling to make a rectangle, pressing the edges together firmly to seal.

4 Lift the pastry on to an oiled baking sheet. Glaze with beaten egg, then pierce a few times with a skewer.

5 Bake on the middle shelf of the oven for 40 minutes, covering with foil after 30 minutes. Leave to cool on the baking sheet, before cutting into slices. Serve garnished with watercress.

Avocado & Smoked Mackerel Salad

Smoked fish and avocado make an unusual but delicious combination.

Serves 4

INGREDIENTS
15 g/½ oz/1 tbsp butter or margarine
½ onion, finely sliced
5 ml/1 tsp mustard seeds
225 g/8 oz smoked mackerel fillet, skinned
  and flaked
30 ml/2 tbsp chopped fresh coriander
2 firm tomatoes, peeled and chopped
30 ml/2 tbsp lemon juice
2 avocados, peeled, stoned and
thinly sliced
½ cucumber, thinly sliced
2 firm tomatoes, thinly sliced
1 green chilli, seeded and finely chopped
salt and freshly ground black pepper

1 Melt the butter or margarine in a frying pan, add the onion and mustard seeds and fry for about 2 minutes until the onion is soft.

2 Add the fish, coriander, tomatoes and 15 ml/1 tbsp lemon juice and cook over a low heat for 2–3 minutes. Remove from the heat and cool.

3 To make the salad, place the avocados in a bowl and sprinkle with the remaining lemon juice. Place the fish mixture in the centre of a plate. Arrange the avocados, cucumber and tomatoes decoratively around the outside of the fish. Sprinkle with the chopped chilli, season and serve.

Sardine & Black Olive Salad

The combined ingredients create a burst of flavour in this delightful dish.

Serves 6

INGREDIENTS
8 large firm ripe tomatoes
1 large red onion
60 ml/4 tbsp wine vinegar
90 ml/6 tbsp good olive oil
18–24 small sardines, grilled or fried
75 g/3 oz/¾ cup pitted black olives,
    drained well
salt and freshly ground black pepper
45 ml/3 tbsp chopped fresh parsley,
    to garnish

1 Slice the tomatoes into 5 mm/¼ in thick slices. Slice the onion thinly. Arrange the tomatoes on a serving plate, then top with the onion.

2 Mix together the wine vinegar, olive oil and seasoning to taste. Spoon over the tomatoes and onions.

3 Top with the sardines and black olives. Sprinkle with the chopped parsley and serve.

Moroccan Tuna Salad

Similar to the classic French *Salade Niçoise,* this dish uses tuna or swordfish steaks steeped in flavoursome *charmoula* marinade before grilling.

Serves 6

INGREDIENTS
900 g/2 lb fresh tuna or swordfish, sliced
    into 2 cm/¾ in steaks
olive oil, for brushing

FOR THE *CHARMOULA*
1 onion
2 garlic cloves
½ bunch fresh parsley
½ bunch fresh coriander
10 ml/2 tsp paprika
45 ml/3 tbsp olive oil
30 ml/2 tbsp white wine vinegar
15 ml/1 tbsp lime or lemon juice

FOR THE SALAD
450 g/1 lb French beans
450 g/1 lb broad beans
1 cos lettuce, separated
450 g/1 lb cherry tomatoes, halved,
    unless very tiny
30 ml/2 tbsp coarsely chopped fresh coriander
3 hard-boiled eggs
45 ml/3 tbsp olive oil
10–15 ml/2–3 tsp lime or lemon juice
½ garlic clove, crushed
175–225 g/6–8 oz/1½–2 cups
    black olives, pitted

1 To make the *charmoula,* place all the ingredients in a food processor, add 45 ml/3 tbsp water and process for 30–40 seconds until finely chopped.

2 Prick the fish steaks all over with a fork, place in a shallow dish and pour over the *charmoula,* turning the fish to coat thoroughly. Cover and leave in a cool place for 2–4 hours.

3 To prepare the salad, cook the French beans and broad beans in boiling salted water until tender. Drain and refresh under cold water. Discard the outer shells from the broad beans and place the broad beans in a large serving bowl with the French beans.

4 Add the lettuce, tomatoes and coriander to the beans. Shell the eggs and cut into eighths. Blend the olive oil, lime or lemon juice and garlic.

5 Preheat the grill and arrange the fish steaks in a grill pan. Brush with the marinade and a little extra olive oil and grill for 5–6 minutes on each side until the fish is tender and flakes easily. Brush with marinade and more olive oil when turning the fish over.

6 Allow the fish to cool a little and then break the steaks into large pieces. Toss into the salad with the olives and dressing. Decorate the Moroccan salad with the eggs and serve.

Thai Scented Fish Salad

For a tropical taste of the Far East, try this delicious fish salad scented with coconut, fruit and warm Thai spices.

Serves 4

INGREDIENTS
350 g/12 oz fillet of red mullet, sea bream
or snapper
1 cos lettuce, separated
½ lollo biondo lettuce, separated
1 papaya or mango, peeled
and sliced
1 pithaya, peeled and sliced
1 large ripe tomato, cut into wedges
½ cucumber, peeled and cut
into batons
3 spring onions, sliced

FOR THE MARINADE
5 ml/1 tsp coriander seeds
5 ml/1 tsp fennel seeds
2.5 ml/½ tsp cumin seeds
5 ml/1 tsp caster sugar
2.5 ml/½ tsp hot chilli sauce
30 ml/2 tbsp olive oil
1 clove garlic, crushed
salt

FOR THE DRESSING
15 ml/1 tbsp creamed coconut
60 ml/4 tbsp groundnut or
safflower oil
finely grated rind and juice of 1 lime
1 red chilli, seeded and
finely chopped
5 ml/1 tsp sugar
45 ml/3 tbsp chopped
fresh coriander

1 Cut the fish into even strips and place on a plate or in a shallow bowl. To make the marinade, crush the coriander, fennel and cumin seeds and mix with the sugar in a small bowl. Add the chilli sauce, oil, garlic and salt and combine.

2 Spread the marinade over the fish, cover and leave to stand in a cool place for at least 20 minutes – longer if you have time.

3 To make the dressing, place the creamed coconut and a pinch of salt in a screw-top jar with 45 ml/3 tbsp boiling water and allow to dissolve. Add the oil, lime rind and juice, red chilli, sugar and chopped fresh coriander. Shake well and set aside.

4 Wash and spin the lettuce leaves. Combine with the papaya or mango, pithaya, tomato, cucumber and spring onions. Toss with the dressing, then distribute among four large plates.

5 Heat a large, non-stick frying pan, add the strips of fish and cook for 5 minutes, turning once. Arrange the cooked fish over the salad and serve immediately.

COOK'S TIP: You can leave the fish in its marinade for up to 8 hours.

Smoked Trout & Noodle Salad

It is important to use ripe, juicy tomatoes for this fresh-tasting salad. For a special occasion you could replace the smoked trout with smoked salmon.

Serves 4

INGREDIENTS
225 g/8 oz somen noodles
2 smoked trout, skinned and boned
2 hard-boiled eggs, shelled and
  coarsely chopped
30 ml/2 tbsp snipped
  fresh chives
lime halves, to serve (optional)

FOR THE DRESSING
6 ripe plum tomatoes
2 shallots, finely chopped
30 ml/2 tbsp tiny capers, rinsed
30 ml/2 tbsp chopped
  fresh tarragon
finely grated rind and juice
  of ½ orange
60 ml/4 tbsp extra virgin
  olive oil
salt and freshly ground
  black pepper

1 To make the dressing, cut the tomatoes in half, discard the cores and cut the flesh into chunks.

COOK'S TIP: Choose tomatoes that are firm, bright in colour and have a matt texture, avoiding any with blotched or cracked skins.

2 Place in a bowl with the shallots, capers, tarragon, orange rind, orange juice and olive oil. Season with salt and pepper and mix well. Leave the dressing to stand at room temperature for 1–2 hours.

3 Cook the noodles in a large saucepan of boiling water until just tender. Drain and rinse under cold running water. Drain well.

4 Toss the cooled noodles with the dressing, then adjust the seasoning to taste. Arrange the dressed noodles on a large serving platter or four individual plates, if preferred.

5 Flake the smoked trout over the noodles, then sprinkle the coarsely chopped eggs and snipped chives over the top. Serve the lime halves on the side, if you like.

First published in 1999 by Hermes House

Hermes House is an imprint of
Anness Publishing Limited
Hermes House
88-89 Blackfriars Road
London SE1 8HA

A CIP catalogue record for this book is available from the British Library

Publisher: Joanna Lorenz
Editor: Valerie Ferguson
Series Designer: Bobbie Colgate Stone
Designer: Andrew Heath
Editorial Reader: Hayley Kerr
Production Controller: Joanna King

Recipes contributed by: Catherine Atkinson, Angela Boggiano, Carla Capalbo, Lesley Chamberlain,
Carole Clements, Trisha Davies, Roz Denny, Matthew Drennan, Sarah Edmonds, Christine France,
Silvano Franco, Rosamund Grant, Judy Jackson, Manisha Kanani, Maggie Pannell,
Katherine Richmond, Liz Trigg, Elizabeth Wolf-Cohen, Jeni Wright.

Photography: Karl Adamson, James Duncan, John Freeman, Ian Garlick, Michelle Garrett,
John Heseltine, Amanda Heywood, Janine Hosegood, David Jordan,
Patrick McLeavey, Thomas Odulate.

1 3 5 7 9 10 8 6 4 2

Notes:
For all recipes, quantities are given in both metric and imperial measures and,
where appropriate, measures are also given in standard cups and spoons.
Follow one set, but not a mixture, because they are
not interchangeable.

Standard spoon and cup measures are level.

1 tsp = 5 ml   1 tbsp = 15 ml

1 cup = 250 ml/8 fl oz

Australian standard tablespoons are 20 ml.
Australian readers should use 3 tsp in place of 1 tbsp for measuring small quantities of gelatine,
cornflour, salt, etc.

Medium eggs are used unless otherwise stated.

Printed and bound in China